Wicca Spells

How To Get Started With Wiccan Spells, Discover The Book Of Shadows, Magic And Spells You Can Use

Respective authors own all copyrights not held by the publisher.

The information herein is offered for informational purposes solely, and is universal as so The presentation of the information is without contract or any type ofguarantee assurance.

The trademarks that are used are without any consent, and the publication of the trademark is without permission or backing by the trademark owner. All trademarks and brands within this book are for clarifying purposes only and are owned by the owners themselves, not affiliated with this document.

Table of Contents

Free Essential Magick Book

Wicca Magick can be a difficult subject to grasp, luckily I have give you many books to get your head around it.

Gain more knowledge! Grab your FREE copy of The Essential Magick Book to help you understand what you need to be a better practitioner

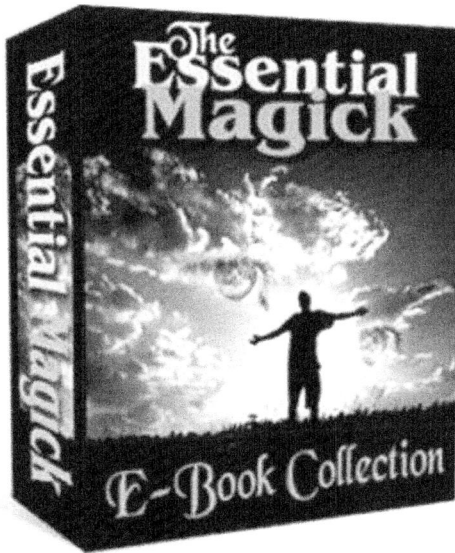

To grab your copy of The Marketing Blue Print visit

http://www.scarlettwrightbooks.com/wiccamagick

How to Practice Magic

Magic is so much more than a man with a pointy hat muttering some arcane chant, or a magician pulling a rabbit out of a hat. Magic is a way of using the natural energy present in the universe to effect change, whether for good or for ill. For Wiccans, who believe that whatever you do comes back to you threefold, magic is a powerful force that is only to be practiced for positive reasons. Wiccans use magic for a variety of reasons, from casting spells for personal success or luck, to reciting an incantation to cure a headache, or even performing magic designed to find their true love. But magic isn't a powerful cure-all, to be used without careful consideration. Magic is something you must think about, carefully weighing the benefits and the possible consequences, before casting so much as a single spell. It should not be the first port of call, but rather should be used as an aid to your normal, mundane, non-magical methods.

Magic only requires that you are able to direct energy toward a goal - but it does not specify how you have to do it. In its simplest form, you don't even need words to cast a spell. Simply focus your mind on what you want, and send the energy of the universe where you need it to go. But many Wiccans feel that magic should be a little more special than that. They find that the act of casting a circle, of handling the ingredients, of chanting ritual words, can serve as an aid to clear and to focus their mind. You have to find the way that works for you best - whatever gets you in the right frame of mind to perform magic. Whether that requires you to purify yourself first, to change into special clothing, to cast a circle and meditate before you begin; or if you think that saying a simple incantation is the best way for you to work your magic, then that's okay too.

As you research spellcasting, you will find that there are a huge variety of spells available. Some spells you find will be elaborate, with lengthy chants and a significant amount of preparation required. Still others may be as simple as a few rhyming lines. Research and practice, and you will soon learn the way in which casting magic works best for you. Some Wiccans may mix and match, performing more elaborate spellcasting during Sabbats, when they will be conducting rituals anyway, but using simpler spells for everyday spellcasting. Wicca is a highly flexible religion, and it is important when working magic to choose what feels right for you.

Wiccans who tap into the magical world are able to use their willpower to direct energy toward a specific goal. To do so requires a great deal of focus, and for this reason meditation is also an important part of magical practice. You have to learn to quiet your mind, to be able to direct all your attention toward spellcasting. More so than the specific words you chant, the herbs or crystals you use, or even where you choose to practice, the key to spellcasting is your focus.

Whenever you decide to cast a spell, you should take a few moments before beginning to calm your mind, until you can bring all of that powerful focus and willpower to bear, to direct the energy to your will. Don't just read the words of the spell - really feel them, feel the power that resonates in them. And even while you recite, keep your reason for casting the spell foremost in your mind. If you're casting a spell to bring about a new job, you must really be focusing on calling that job to you. If you let your mind wander, if you lose focus, then the energy won't know where to go. Rather than directing it purposefully toward a specific goal, you'll only be pushing it vaguely in that general direction.

Intention is another important part of spellcasting. It's even possible to work magic without casting a spell at all, with just using your intention and willpower to direct the energy. Many cultures around the world believe in the evil eye - that it's possible to direct negative energy at a person, and bring sickness, injury, or bad luck just by looking at them. If the intention is the key when it comes to working magic, then simply by having strong negative feelings about another person it would be all too easy to cause them harm. This type of magic can cause what is known as a "psychic attack" - where negative energy is directed toward a person to cause them harm. Some may choose to practice this type of magic deliberately, disregarding the Threefold Law and the fundamental belief that you should harm none, and using their magic for malicious purposes, but it is also possible to psychically attack someone unintentionally, simply by having strong feelings of anger, jealousy and envy. Thoughts have power, just as much as words do.

When casting a spell, it is very important that your intention is clear, and your mind is focused. If you think you're casting a general spell to bring love into your life, but then your mind keeps wandering toward your ex who you haven't quite gotten over, then you might unintentionally find yourself drawing them back into your life instead (and interfering with their free will in the process). Or you may cast a spell to achieve a promotion at work, but what you're actually thinking is "I deserve that promotion, but I know they're going to give it to that other person, even though they don't work as hard as I do!" Without realizing it, you are directing negative energy toward that other person, and you may end up causing them harm. Before you start practicing magic, it is very important to train your mind, through meditation and visualization, so that you are able to focus on your aim without distraction, and without other thoughts intruding.

Another thing to bear in mind is that, when it comes to magic, the expression "be careful what you wish for" is very true. Every spell you cast has consequences. If you cast a spell to increase your wealth, think about where that wealth is going to come from. Yes, of course it could be something fairly harmless like winning the lottery or being given a raise at work. But it could also be receiving an inheritance after someone you care about has passed away. A spell to attract love could draw someone to you against their will, or you may find that they love you a lot more than you love them. Find yourself having a difficult day at work and decide to cast a spell to remove stress? Well, if you walk in the next day and find you've been fired, technically the stress of that job has been removed. Magic should always be used with caution. Even if your intention is not to harm anyone, you may find that your spell does have negative consequences. And always remember, whatever you do comes back to you threefold.

When you first start learning magic, it may seem very daunting. You see spells with lengthy chants, calling for all sorts of exotic ingredients that you've never even heard of. But don't panic. Yes, there are spells that are complicated, but there are also a great number of spells that are very simple. As you research, try to find a few spells that only require incantations, or only use very basic ingredients that you may already have in your kitchen, or that are very easy to pick up in a trip to the store. You can use these simple spells to get a feeling for spellcasting, learning what works for you when it comes to magic. There's no point rushing out and buying expensive crystals, only to then learn that you find that using crystals in spellwork simply doesn't work for you. Over time, as you grow in experience and as you build up a store of ingredients, you will find it easier to progress onto more complicated spells, if you so choose.

Of course, there's no rule saying you must work elaborate spells. If, in your practice, you find that a particular type of magic seems to work really well for you, then feel free to continue using that form. If you find you like using quick and simple incantations, because on the longer incantations your mind tends to wander and you lose focus, then there is nothing wrong with using only shorter incantations. If you find that candle magic works really well for you, then continue using candles in your spellcasting. There are no hard and fast rules when it comes to magic - you need to find the form of spellcasting that works best for you.

As you find the spells that work for you, you should begin writing them in your Book of Shadows. Note down the ones that work, as well as any variations to the spell that you have made - perhaps you did not have the herbs that they called for, so substituted ones with similar properties, and then found that the spell worked better than you expected. Or perhaps it didn't work at all, and then you could make a note reminding you not to use those substitute herbs next time.

Some spells you may cast only once - if your spell to attract your soulmate works, then you probably won't need to cast it again. But for some spells (like spells to cure a headache), you will probably be using over and over again. Over time, you will find that you remember the spells very easily, and you won't need to refer to your Book of Shadows at all. But it's always a good idea to write them down. Your Book of Shadows, as well as serving as a reference book, is also a diary of your spiritual journey, and even when you have your headache spell memorized, it's still interesting to be able to look back and see how far you have progressed since you learned that spell, and how much your spellcasting has evolved since you first wrote it down.

It's also useful to write the magical correspondences in your Book of Shadows. As you continue to practice magic, you will find that they start to come more naturally to you, and without even looking you will know that a red candle is used for love magic, while a blue candle is used for healing magic. But with such a vast array of herbs and crystals that are used in magic, it can be difficult to remember them all - and if you're looking to substitute a herb in one of your spells, it's good to be able to look in your Book of Shadows and see that lavender and mint can both be used to promote good sleep, and so you know you can try substituting mint because you've run out of lavender.

This book is designed to give you a feel for practicing magic. The spells in this book are relatively simple, requiring only a few basic ingredients, as well as being quick to cast. This isn't an exercise book - you don't need to work your way through each and every spell. Just use the ones that you need, and make sure you really do need them before you begin casting.

Love Spells

When people think of magic, often the first thing that comes to mind is casting love spells. After all, what could be more appealing than the idea of using magic to bring a little romance into your life? But while it is the most appealing, it is also the one with which you must exercise the most care. While there is nothing wrong with using magic to attract love into your life, you must be careful if you're using a spell to attract a specific person. Because if you cast a spell on someone to make them love you, aren't you harming them by taking away their free will? You should also consider whether you think it's okay to work magic on someone without their consent. It's one thing to cast a healing spell for someone you love, but it's quite another to use magic to change the way someone feels about you. Perhaps the better way is to cast magic to improve yourself - to make yourself feel more confident, more outgoing, more attractive. Or cast a general spell to attract love into your life, without specifying where that love will come from.

Red is the color most commonly associated with love - even those who do not practice Wicca consider this color to be the most romantic and passionate of all. Pink can also be used when you are casting a spell for relationships, although this color tends to be more often used with platonic relationships and friendships than with true romantic love. Apples and apple seeds are often used in magical workings related to love, due to their association with the Goddess Aphrodite (in Greek legend, it was an apple given to the Goddess Aphrodite that caused the Trojan war). Lavender, vanilla, and jasmine are also used, most often in the form of essential oils. If you want to use something from your kitchen cupboard, try cinnamon, cloves, or fennel. The most obvious flower to use in love rituals is, of course, the rose, but you could also use carnations for relationship spells. If you like to work with crystals, rose quartz works very well for any sort of love magic (especially if you are casting a spell to increase your self-esteem, to attract love by first loving yourself).

A Simple Love Spell

Requiring no tools, candles, or herbs, this simple incantation can help to draw love into your life.

You will need:
Your willpower

Making sure that the desire to attract love is foremost in your mind, and your thoughts are not wandering, say:

My heart is open wide
Let the universe be my guide
I ask for love, let me receive
In my heart I do believe

Focus on keeping your heart and mind open, and on receiving whatever messages the universe chooses to send you. The one who you are meant to love may not be who you expect - after all, you didn't wish for a specific person, you just wanted to attract love into your life.

A New Moon Love Spell

The new moon is a time for new beginnings - what better time to start a new relationship, or to cast a spell for new love?

You will need:

A white candle

Amethyst and rose quartz

Sage

Rosemary

Before you begin, you should purify yourself. This spell is about new beginnings - you don't want to bring the baggage of old relationships and old habits into the spell. Take a bath, and take some time to meditate to calm yourself and clear your mind. You want to leave any past negativity behind so that you can begin anew.

Light the candle, and use the sage and rosemary to smudge your ritual area. You want everything to be purified and cleansed before you begin. Once the space is cleansed, you can begin.

Light the candle and sit in front of it, holding the amethyst and the rose quartz. Rose quartz brings new love; amethyst is a powerful stone for purification. As you look at the white candle, feel yourself leaving your old relationships behind. Whatever experiences, good or bad, you had are now in the past - they no longer affect you. Whatever type of person you normally attract no longer matters. You are starting afresh in order to begin a new relationship unsullied by the events of the past. As you look into the flame and as you feel your past experiences being unburdened, say:

As I see the new moon rise

Soaring high into the skies

I am reborn, I am renewed

Upon my past I no longer brood

As the light of the Lady shines upon me

Bound by my mistakes I no longer will be

I call upon love to fill my heart

As the moon rises my new life will start

As the candle burns down, see your past relationships disappearing, feel yourself being purified and cleansed, and leave the circle feeling refreshed, renewed, and ready to begin again.

To Attract a Lover

Another easy way to attract love to you is by making a charm bag. Charm bags are frequently used in spells of attraction, and can also be used to attract fortune and wealth just by changing a few key ingredients.

You will need:

A red bag (or some red fabric)

Rose petals

Lavender

Jasmine essential oil

A piece of rose quartz

Red ribbon

Take a moment to imagine love filling your life. Focus on calling love to you as you place each item in the bag. Sprinkle the jasmine oil on the outside of the bag, and say:

Across the land and the deep blue sea

With this charm I call love to me

Seal the bag (either by sewing it shut or tying it with a red ribbon), and carry it with you until love enters your life and the spell is complete.

Knot Love Spell

Knot magic is one of the simplest, yet most powerful forms of magic there is. All you need is a piece of string and your willpower, and you can work almost any spell imaginable. Try using this spell to attract new love into your life.

You will need:

A piece of string (preferably red or pink)

Hold the piece of string in your hand and take a few moments to visualize your ideal lover. Don't think of a specific person - instead, think of the qualities you would want your lover to have. Imagine the two of you falling in love, and imagine what your relationship will be like.

Keep this image in mind as you tie the first knot in the string. As you tie the knot, say:

Venus, Freya, Aphrodite, Goddesses Three
Bring new love to my life, so mote it be

Continue to visualize and repeat the incantation as you tie eight more knots in the string.

Keep the string with you until your spell is successful, and you find your lover. If at any point you wish to end the relationship, take the string and untie the knots one by one, saying:

For the one who holds my heart
I wish this love now to depart

Make Love Grow

A simple yet powerful spell, using the power of the Earth to make your love grow. This spell will take some time to work, but will allow your love to grow naturally.

You will need:
Some seeds (apple seeds work particularly well)
A plant pot and some compost

Take the seeds in your hand and hold them while thinking of the one you love. Think of your relationship, feel the love you have inside of you. When you are ready, take the seeds and plant them in the compost, saying this simple incantation:

As this plant grows to the sky
May our love never die

Look after the plant and keep it well watered. As the seeds begin to germinate and grow, your love should grow ever stronger.

To Stop Jealousy

So now you've found your perfect partner, but you can't stop the green-eyed monster from rising. You're so afraid of losing them, you're jumping at shadows, imaging that everyone out there is trying to steal your partner away. This simple spell uses herbs associated with love, fidelity, and loyalty, and can help to quell your suspicions. But use with caution - you don't want to take away your partner's free will. And bear in mind, your suspicions may not be groundless - use your common sense, and don't try and use magic to save a relationship that is struggling. Don't be so desperate for love that you blind yourself to your partner's actions. But if your partner is otherwise loving and attentive, and it is only your jealousy causing you to suffer, then you can try using this spell.

You will need:

Sprigs of rosemary, basil, parsley, and thyme

Pink string or ribbon

Focus on your jealousy and suspicion, and tie the herbs together in a bundle. Say:

Jealousy, envy, I cast you out

Inside my heart there is no doubt

My love is true, my faith is strong

I have found the place where I belong

Once this is done, you should place the bundle somewhere the knot cannot come undone - bury it if you must.

To Find Your Soulmate

Perhaps you are tired of jumping from relationship to relationship, and never quite finding what you need. What you really want is to find your soulmate, that one special person who is destined to be with you.

You will need:

Some paper, torn into small pieces

A pen or pencil

A body of water (lake, river, or sea)

At the new moon, take some time to meditate on what your soulmate would be like. Think of their most important qualities - should they have a sense of humor? Do they need to be a great cook? Should they be kind, compassionate, and thoughtful? Write all these qualities down on pieces of paper. When you are sure that you are ready, take the paper to a stream or lake. Cast the pieces in one at a time, and as you do so, say:

Spirits of the water, keepers of emotion

I call upon you to take my desires

Bring me what my soul requires

Someone for my heart's devotion

A partner to help me weather life's trials

A (man/woman) who brings me smiles

Take my wishes to the sea

Find the one who's right for me

Watch the pieces of paper as they bob away and know that you are casting your wish out into the universe, and if the time is right, the universe will send you that which you most desire.

To Love Yourself

They say that the best way to make someone find you attractive is to be confident in yourself. Sometimes the best way to find love is to love yourself first. By putting that sort of positive energy out into the universe, you can only attract positive energy - and love - unto yourself.

You will need:

Ginger

Citrine

A purple candle

Light the candle and sprinkle a pinch of ginger into the flame (carefully - you don't want to sprinkle too much ginger and put the flame out, otherwise the spell won't work). Sit in front of the candle holding the citrine, and look at the flame. As you sit, meditate on all of your good qualities. You might find it difficult at first - people often find it easier to criticize themselves than to praise - but persevere. As you think these positive thoughts, you are charging the citrine with positive energy and self-love. Say:

I look now inside my heart
To love myself, I will now start
I see that I am good, I am kind
To my strengths I am not blind

When you are ready, extinguish the candle. Continue to carry the citrine around with you and feel your self-confidence increase.

To Make Yourself More Desirable

Brimming with self-confidence, yet still struggling to attract a lover? Try this spell to increase your desirability and attractiveness.

You will need:
Four pieces of rose quartz

Rose essential oil

Rose petals

A red candle

Use the essential oil and rose petals to create a circle. Place a piece of rose quartz at the four cardinal points of the circle. When you are finished, stand at the center of the circle and light the candle. Then recite the following incantation:

Like the moon high up in the sky

My beauty no one can deny

One look at me and hearts soon will sigh

Love no longer to pass me by

Repeat the incantation twice, feeling yourself grow more beautiful and more desirable with every word you speak. When you have finished, open the circle and go out into the world knowing that love will soon be coming your way.

Find Out Your Lover's Initials

This ritual is best performed at Samhain, but it can be conducted at any time of the year. Simple to perform, yet extremely effective.

You will need:

An apple

A sharp knife

Peel the apple in one continuous unbroken piece. Holding the peel carefully in your left hand, and focusing all your mind on love, turn around clockwise three times, then toss the peel over your left shoulder. When it lands, it will form the first letter of your future lover's name. If the peel breaks upon landing, it means your relationship will be difficult.

How to Scry For Your Lover

Another ritual that is best performed at Samhain, this simple ritual uses divination to show you the face of your lover. The most popular way to do this is to use a mirror, although it is also possible to use a bowl of water.

You will need:

A mirror (or a bowl of water)

A red or white candle

In a darkened room, take a few moments to center and calm yourself, then light the candle. As you look at its flame, think about love and what it means to you. Do not think too much about your ideal partner - the aim of this spell isn't to draw a particular person to you, but rather to see the person who is right for you. And try to focus on what you want - if your mind drifts, and you start worrying about work or exams, you might find yourself seeing your boss or your teacher instead of your future lover!

When you are ready, look up at the mirror (or look down into the bowl of water). You should see someone standing behind you, another face in the water besides your own. Try not to jump - this was the intention of the spell, after all. You may only catch a brief glimpse before the face is gone, but try to remember who you have seen. It may be someone you know, or someone you have never met before - but this person is destined to be your lover.

To Banish an Unwanted Admirer

Sometimes you find that someone loves you, but you do not reciprocate their love. In order to persuade this admirer to look elsewhere, it might be useful to cast a little spell.

You will need:

A piece of string (red or black)

Holding the piece of string, spend a few moments thinking of your unwanted admirer. Focus and channel all their unwanted attentions into the string. When the moment is right, tie a knot into the string and say:

(Name) as you send your affections to me

I bind them into this knot

So that I may be free

Place the string in a safe place - the spell will only work so long as the knot is unbroken - and your admirer should direct their attentions elsewhere.

To Return Lost Love

Use this spell with caution - after all, there is usually a good reason for lost love, and it may simply be time to let the relationship go. But if you feel that the relationship could work, and deserves another chance, you could try this simple spell.

You will need:

A piece of red fabric

A ribbon or piece of string (red)

A piece of your hair

A photo of your ex

A red candle

This spell should be cast during the waxing moon. Light the candle and, holding the photo in front of you, say the following:

What was lost should be returned

A love like this has surely been earned

Let the bonds of love be rekindled

Let the fire be stoked that now has dwindled

The love I feel inside my heart

Burns ever brighter since we've been apart

Find my love and return (him/her) to me

As I will so mote it be

Place the photo and lock of your hair into the fabric, and tie the bundle tightly shut with the ribbon. Allow the candle to burn itself out - as the flame grows ever lower, imagine that your ex is returning to you. Keep the bundle somewhere safe - if it is opened, the spell will be undone.

To End a Relationship

Breakups can be difficult. Doubts, lingering feelings, and sadness are common. To make a clean break, you can perform this simple candle spell to cleanse yourself of the old relationship.

You will need:

A piece of paper

A pen or pencil

A candle (preferably white)

This spell is most powerful when performed under a waning moon. On the piece of paper, write the name of your ex. Spend a few moments thinking about your relationship, both the good and the bad. When you are ready, light the candle and place the piece of paper into the flame. Allow the paper to burn, and visualize letting go of the relationship. Say:

A love that once burned so bright

A light extinguished, feelings dwindle

This relationship I will not rekindle

Remove these feelings out of sight

When you are done, extinguish the candle.

How to Heal a Broken Heart

So your relationship hasn't worked out, for whatever reason, and now you find yourself alone. It can be difficult to move on while you are still holding onto feelings for your ex. While only time can truly heal a broken heart, magic can help to ease some of your suffering.

You will need:

A piece of black string

Knot magic is perhaps most powerful when it is used to bind something. Here, you will be binding your old feelings for your

25

ex, as well as your feelings of heartbreak and sadness, and banishing them from your life. This spell may be painful, but it will help.

First you will need to bring all those horrible feelings to the surface. While holding the string, sit and think of your ex. Think of the love you shared and the relationship you had, and allow yourself to feel all the sadness and loss and grief at the ending of your relationship. You are transferring all of this negative energy into the piece of string. When your feelings are so strong you cannot bear it anymore, tie a knot into the string and say:

I give you my sorrow

I give you my pain

And by tomorrow

I will be whole again

Continue this process of tying knots and chanting eight more times, and feel the pain inside of you diminish with each knot you tie. By the time you are finished, you should feel lighter and calmer. Bury the string - this is one spell you won't want to undo.

Spells for Protection, Banishing and Healing

Sometimes your life does not go exactly as you planned, and you find yourself needing to use magic for your own protection. Perhaps you did a little divination and now you feel an unwelcome presence in your house - or perhaps that unwelcome presence is a person whose negativity you'd like to remove from your life. Perhaps you're going through a stressful period in your life and you'd like a little magical boost. Or maybe you're suffering from ill health, and you're wondering if magic might be able to help you. The second most common types of spells cast by Wiccans are spells for banishing (whether that is banishing ill health, negativity, or the habit of smoking) and for protection (whether from psychic attack, negative energy, or even burglary).

Non-Wiccans may associate black with darkness and devil worship, but Wiccans most frequently use black in banishing spells. White, obviously, is associated with purity and so is most often used for protection and for cleansing. Light blue is often used for healing magic, while dark blue is used when the healing is for a mental ailment, rather than a physical one. Sage is a very powerful herb, and as well as being used to cleanse a space, it can also be used in banishing a malevolent spirit. Eucalyptus oil can also be used for cleansing, and for making your home smell pleasant. Another strong-smelling herb, garlic, can be used for protection, and is particularly effective when hung in the doorway of your home. An aloe plant in the home can also provide protection. Crystals are very powerful when used for protection and for healing. Something as simple as carrying a piece of hematite or tiger's eye can protect you from psychic attacks and dispel negative energy. And if you're looking for healing, try using crystal quartz.

A Simple Protection Spell

This is the easiest, quickest protection spell you can cast. You can use it for when you feel uneasy, when you feel anxious for no reason, or you can use it for protection against a more specific threat. Perhaps you feel that someone is directing negativity your way, and you want a quick way to separate yourself from that negative energy, giving you time to find a more detailed banishing spell. Memorize this spell, and you'll always have it at the ready.

You will need:
Your willpower

This spell is very simple. Close your eyes, and envision yourself being surrounded by a circle of pure white light. This white light then begins to spread, surrounding you in a sphere of pure positive energy. If you wish, you may say:

With this circle, I surround myself with light

I am safe inside, none may enter

Inside I wait, out of sight

Safe in the Mother's love, at the center

Repeat the spell a few more times, until you begin to feel calmer. Know that you are safe inside this shield until you choose to end the spell. To end the spell, visualize that white light slowly dissipating, and simply say:

The circle is open

This spell is very similar to how you cast a circle when performing a ritual, but the focus here is on protecting yourself, rather than protecting your ritual space.

A Simple Healing Spell

There are many ways to heal - some using crystals, some using herbs - but you can cast a basic healing spell using nothing but your willpower.

You will need:

Your will power

Begin by closing your eyes and grounding yourself. Then imagine a pure, white, healing light filling your body, starting at your head and moving slowly down through your body. If there are any specific areas that need treating, allow the light to hover there for a few moments. Feel the light warming and soothing as it fills you. Allow the light to continue on its journey until it passes out through your feet. Feel how you are relaxed and refreshed. Take a few moments to enjoy this feeling before you open your eyes.

A Spell to Cleanse Your Home

You may like to conduct this ritual as part of a spring cleaning, to cleanse your home both physically and spiritually. Or you may feel that there is a negative energy in your house that you would like to remove. Or perhaps you have just moved into a new house, and would like to remove all traces of the previous occupants. It never hurts to conduct a cleansing ritual, and you may find that the house feels a little lighter even if you hadn't noticed any negativity present.

You will need:

Sage or salt water

A heat-resistant bowl

Some matches or a lighter

You can either use a bundle of sage (but be careful not to burn your fingers!) or you can use dried sage. If you are using a bundle of sage, use your matches to light one end until it is smoking gently. If you are using dried sage, sprinkle some into the bowl before lighting it. With the smoking sage, move around your house, making sure to visit each room in turn. As you walk, imagine the smoke blowing through the house, removing the negative influences and leaving purity in its wake. As you walk, say:

With scent of sage and power of air
I purge the negativity from my home
As I walk now, here and there
Let no more evil within these walls roam

If you have neighbors who might object to the scent of burning sage (which can smell a little like another, slightly more illegal, green herb), you can conduct a similar ritual using salt water. As you pass through the house, carry a bowl of salt water and sprinkle some in each room, making sure to get into all the corners. If you're using salt water, say:

By strength of Earth and might of Water
I purge the negativity from my home
As I walk, my steps do not falter
Let no more evil within these walls roam

Once you have finished cleansing the house, you may wish to light a white candle to complete the cleansing ritual.

To Banish a Spirit

Sage and salt water are also frequently used to banish a troublesome spirit. Use this spell with caution - if you've already asked the spirit nicely to leave and they've refused, then you're dealing with a more malevolent spirit, and they may not react too well to being forced to leave.

You will need:

Sage or salt water

A heat-resistant bowl

Some matches or a lighter

Before you begin, cast a simple protection spell to surround yourself with a protective white light. Also make sure that no one else is in the house - you don't want someone else to get hurt accidentally. Once this is done, light your sage or begin sprinkling salt water and move through the house, saying:

Unwilling spirit, unwelcome guest

I banish you now, from my home and my life

Continue walking through the house until you have visited every room, and the house feels clean. You may want to place a line of salt at all doors and windows to prevent the spirit from returning.

To Give Up a Bad Habit

It can be difficult to change a bad habit. Whether it's smoking, drinking too much, or biting your nails, it takes a lot of effort and willpower to change your ways. If you're finding it difficult, why not try giving your efforts a little magical boost?

You will need:

A piece of string (preferably orange)

A black candle

This spell is best cast during a waning moon. While holding the string, take some time to think of the habit you want to change. Spend some time visualizing it - imagine how it feels to smoke a cigarette, or picture biting your nails. Imagine the craving, the desperate desire that comes when you try to break the habit. Now imagine the craving is passing into the string. Feel it leaving your body, and moving into the thread in your hands. When you feel the last of the craving leave your body, tie three firm knots into the string. Now the craving is trapped in that piece of string. To complete the spell, and to ensure that the craving can never return, light the candle and say the following:

I free myself now of this terrible addiction

No more am I plagued by this affliction

No more to suffer, now I am free

As I will it, so mote it be

Now burn the string in the flame of the candle. This ensures that the knots can never come undone, and that your craving will not return.

A Spell for Crystal Healing

Crystals are powerful stores of magical energy, and can be used to amplify the effects of your spells. Try using crystals for healing particularly stubborn ailments - you'll be surprised at the added boost that a crystal can provide.

You will need:

A piece of clear quartz

Holding the clear quartz in one hand, focus on charging it with your energy. Visualize its purpose - fill it with light and healing energy. While you are charging it with energy, recite this simple spell:

Crystal of power, holder of light

To heal this ailment, I need your aid

To overcome this illness's might

I need your help to make it fade

Once the crystal is charged, you can carry it with you, focusing its energy upon the ailment or area of your body that needs healing. Or you can give it to a friend or loved one, and leave it to work its magic on them.

A Simple Spell for Calming

The power of crystals can also be used for mental healing. Even something as simple as relieving anxiety, or reducing stress, can be achieved using nothing more than a crystal.

You will need:

A piece of amethyst

Choose a time when you are relaxed - you don't want to charge this crystal with any negative energy. Meditate to further calm yourself, until you are centered and grounded, and your mind is still. Take the crystal and hold it in your hands, and allow your calm energy to fill the crystal. Crystals are very good at holding power - once you have charged the crystal, you will be able to use it to calm yourself many times before it will need cleansing and recharging. You can also say:

My mind is still, my thoughts calm
Unbroken water, quiet seas

I look ahead without a qualm

My fears and worries are at ease

Once the crystal is full of energy, you can carry it with you and simply hold it in your hand and feel its energy whenever you are feeling stressed or anxious. Simple, yet effective!

A Spell to Cure a Headache

Before reaching for the painkillers, why not try this quick and easy spell to release the tension and remove your headache?

You will need:

A piece of string (preferably black, but any color will work)

To transfer the tension in your head to the string, tie a loose knot in the string and say:

Pain that grips my head

I pass you now into this thread

Repeat this until you have tied four knots in the thread. You may still feel the tension in your head at this point, but that's okay. The next step will be to release that tension, both from the string and from your head. Working in reverse, move back down the string to each knot in turn. Hopefully you haven't tied them too tightly, because now you're going to have to undo them. Take the first knot and undo it, visualizing the tension flowing away, and say:

Untangled from my body
Unwoven from this thread
The pain you now embody
Return not to my head

As you untie each knot in turn, you should feel the pain in your head begin to ease. A similar spell can be used to bind any pain into a knot and then release it, you simply have to change the words of the spell.

Let this cord now feel my pain
Let its threads now take the strain

Then, when unknotting it, say:

I release this pain
It does not remain

Carry a piece of string of you and, when you feel a headache coming on, try this spell. You'll be surprised at how effective it can be.

A Spell to Protect Against Burglars

This spell is designed to prevent those who would harm you from entering your home. Of course, it's no substitute for locking your front door, but this magical barrier can help to deter burglars.

You will need:

A clean, empty jar (with a lid)

Nails and screws (preferably rusty)

Salt

A piece of your hair (or some nail clippings)

Vinegar

A few mint leaves

Hot chili powder

Some black string

Place the jar in front of you, and have the other ingredients on hand. Say the following incantation:

I call upon the elements four

Nothing evil shall pass this door

Spirit of Earth, I summon you now

Add a handful of salt, then continue:

I call upon the elements now
Into my home, nothing evil allow
Spirit of Air, I summon you now

Add the mint leaves, then continue:

Spirits of nature, hear my call
Nothing evil may enter at all
Spirit of Fire, I summon you now

Add a sprinkle of hot chili powder, then continue:

Spirits of nature, heed my cry
Evil is banished from my house hereby
Spirit of Water, I summon you now

Pour the vinegar into the jar until it is almost full, then continue:

I call upon the Divine
Mother Goddess, Great Horned God
None shall harm that which is mine

Add the lock of your hair, or the nail clippings (or you can even spit into the jar if you prefer), then continue:

With these spikes I build a wall

Barring entry to my hall

Let them grow sharp like the thorns of a rose

Allowing entry only to those I chose

Carefully add the nails and screws, or other sharp objects, into the jar. Screw the lid onto the jar, then very carefully shake the jar to combine all the ingredients. Once they are combined, take the string and wind it around the jar. Tie three knots, and as you tie each knot say:

With this string I bind

All those who would do me harm

I bar all entry to those unkind

Let this jar now be my charm

No evil now shall enter here

Bury the jar outside of your front door - or, if this isn't possible, you should store it inside somewhere near the front door. Now your home should be safe against all negative incursions - whether that be burglars, negative entities, or persistent door-to-door salesmen.

To Protect Yourself Against Psychic Attack

A psychic attack is when someone, whether intentionally or not, sends negative energy in your direction. This could be deliberate, in the form of a curse or evil eye, or perhaps someone is simply wishing you ill. Or it may even be that someone is angry with you and is unintentionally sending negative energy your way. The symptoms can include feeling drained of energy, a general feeling of unease, and feeling like there's a dark cloud over you that just won't go away. You may feel irritable, anxious, and dizzy, or suffer from a sudden headache, nausea, or body aches. If these symptoms occur frequently, or if they strike you out of the blue with no apparent cause, then you may be experiencing a psychic attack.

You are more vulnerable to a psychic attack if you're feeling rundown anyway, so it's important to take care of your physical health. You may also be more susceptible if you are a sensitive person who is very receptive to the emotions of others.

If you think you are experiencing a psychic attack, there are several things you can do to protect yourself. In the short term, you can cast a simple protection spell, casting a circle of light around yourself to cut off the attack. But it can be very draining to maintain this circle for long periods of time. You can choose to either create a more permanent shield, or to redirect the negative energy toward your attacker (but this could be considered as doing harm, even if you are only trying to defend yourself, so use with extreme caution and only as a last resort).

To create a shield, you will need:

Tiger's eye

Sage

A heatproof bowl

A white candle

Cast a circle and light the candle. Sit in front of the candle and look at the flame as you calm and center yourself. As you meditate, take a moment to look at your aura. You may be able to see certain areas look dimmed or blackened. This shows you where the attack is eating away at your defenses. Now focus on the candle again, and feel yourself surrounded by a bubble of pure white light. When you feel safe and secure inside this bubble, take the sage and light it until it is smoking, then place it in the bowl. Taking the tiger's eye in your hands, pass it through the rising smoke several times to purify it. Say:

Healing light, purifying smoke

Charge this crystal with your energy

Protect me from harm I did not provoke

Create a shield to surround me

Surround me with your light

Protect me now with all your might

Carry the tiger's eye around with you to protect yourself from future psychic attacks.

If you are sure that this was a deliberate attack, and you are willing to risk potentially causing harm to another, you can as a last resort try reflecting the negative energy back to its sender.

For this spell, you will need:

A mirror

A black candle

A lock of your hair

A fireproof bowl

In a darkened room, sit in front of the mirror and light the candle. Take the lock of your hair and hold it in the flame until it burns, and say:

Those who send harm unto me

From your negative influence I am free

Place the hair into the bowl to allow it to continue to burn, then look into the mirror. Imagine all those negative thoughts aimed at you striking the mirror and bouncing back off again, and say:

The harm you have sent unto me

I return to you now, so mote it be

Continue to visualize the negative energy reflecting off the mirror, and repeat the chant twice more. You should immediately begin to feel the effects of the psychic attack lessening. But bear in mind, this spell could bring you negative repercussions, so use with care.

A Spell to Remove Obstacles

Is there something standing between you and your goals? Perhaps you would like a pay raise, but you're too afraid to ask. Or you want to exercise, but lack the time and the willpower. Maybe you dream of traveling the world, but you're terrified to take that first step. Try this simple spell to sweep aside any obstacles and allow you to achieve your dreams.

You will need:

A broom

Find a room in your house that is clear and relatively free of obstructions. Or if you have a space outside where you can sweep, you can cast this spell there. Take a few moments to really think about your goal - what do you want to achieve? Then think about what's stopping you, what's standing in your way. As you think about these obstacles, begin to sweep from right to left in long, clean strokes and walk slowly forwards, sweeping as you go. Imagine that you are sweeping away those obstacles and say:

The path in front of me is clear

I step forwards, I have no fear

My path lies open at my feet

I step ahead, my dreams to meet

Continue sweeping and reciting the spell, and feel all your hesitations melting away. Know that when you try to achieve your goal now, there will be nothing that stands in your way.

A Spell for Sleep

Everyone has trouble sleeping from time to time. Rather than reaching for the sleeping pills, why not try making a simple charm bag to aid in restfulness?

You will need:

A pale blue bag (or fabric to make a bag)

A pink ribbon

Lavender

Mint

Passionflower oil

Place the lavender and mint into the bag, and say:

Guardians of the world of sleep

As I lie here counting sheep

I wish only to enter your domain

Listen now, hear my refrain

Sprinkle passionflower oil on the bag and tie it shut. Place it underneath your pillow and you should experience calm, restful sleep.

A Spell to Banish Nightmares

Perhaps what is stopping you from having a calm, restful night's sleep is that you have nightmares whenever you close your eyes. Don't worry - there's a spell for that too!

You will need:

A white candle

A candle holder

Lavender essential oil

A little bit of salt water

Light the candle. Walk counter-clockwise around the room where you sleep and sprinkle the lavender oil, repeating:

Out, demons of the night

I cast you out

Continue walking counter-clockwise around the room, this time sprinkling the salt water, and repeating:

Out, thieves of sleep
I cast you out

Pick up the candle and make one final counter-clockwise circle of the room, repeating:

Out, bringers of fear
I cast you out

Before you extinguish the candle, sprinkle a little of the lavender oil on your pillow. Now you will have a restful night's sleep, free of any fear.

To Undo a Spell

Perhaps you have cast a spell that did not have the desired effect, or perhaps after you've cast it, you realized that your intention was ill. Don't worry - it's relatively simple to undo a spell that you have cast.

You will need:
Any materials you used for the spell
A white candle

A fireproof bowl

If the spell you cast used knot magic, it's very easy to undo. All you have to do is to untie the knots, and say:

The spell that was cast

Let it now be undone

The spell has passed

No longer begun

If the spell you cast did not use knot magic, then light the white candle. One by one, begin to burn any items you used for the spell, saying:

Spirit of Fire, I ask of thee

Undo the magic, unwind this spell

Free the energy, let all be well

As I ask, so mote it be

Repeat this until all the items have been burned, then extinguish the candle. Your magical working should now be undone.

A Spell to Remove Stress

When you're feeling overwhelmed, when stress really feels like it's getting the better of you, you can use magic to calm your mind and release your anxiety.

You will need:
An open area (preferably a park)
A windy day
A dandelion

You will need to be outside for this spell to work. A park is ideal - as well as being a good source of dandelions, it also allows you to take a moment to reconnect with nature. When you are ready, pick a dandelion. Hold it in your hands for a few moments, and imagine all the stress moving out of you and into the dandelion. Hold the dandelion away from you, and let the wind take the seeds. If it's not windy, you can blow the seeds away, and feel the stress moving down your breath and out through the dandelion. See your stress riding the seeds, being carried away from you by the breeze. Say:

Spirit of wind, breath of air
Carry my troubles elsewhere

Stand for a few moments, close your eyes, and take some deep breaths. Feel the nature all around you, and feel your stress melting away.

A Spell to Banish Debt

Best performed at the waning moon, this spell will help you to find a way to clear your debt, and help you to manage your finances better.

You will need:

A black candle

A white candle

A green candle

Small pieces of paper and a pen/pencil

A knife

A fireproof bowl

Before you begin, take a moment to carve the word "debt" on one side of the black and white candles. Then on the papers, write your debts - perhaps you have a car loan you can't pay off, or a mortgage you are struggling with. Maybe you have a personal or payday loan and the interest is crippling you. Whatever your debt, write it down, and write down the amount that you owe. Write each one twice, one copy for each inscribed candle.

Now you are ready to begin.

Light the candles, and begin to burn the pieces of pap
your debt in the flame of the black candle. As you burn
piece, you should say:

By power of the waning moon
By light of the banishing candle
I cast this debt out of my life
I ask the universe to grant this boon
My money woes I cannot handle
Rid me of financial strife

When you have finished burning the paper in the black candle,
you should repeat the process with the white candle. As you
burn each piece, you should say:

By the light of the waning moon
By the purity of this flame
Release me now of this burden
I beseech you to grant this boon
I am free of this debt, I now proclaim
My financial future now is certain

When you have finished burning the paper in the white candle,
you should light the green candle. There are no papers to burn
this time - you should simply look into the flame of the candle,
and say:

Light of prosperity, shine on me

Goddess of Fortune, I look to thee

Bring me wealth, prosperity, security

Bring me safety and financial surety.

Allow the candles to burn until they extinguish themselves. As they burn, imagine leaving your debts behind, and see your new financial future ahead of you.

Spells for Luck, Fortune and Success

The third most popular types of spells are those to bring prosperity. This may be financial prosperity, success at work and in business, or simply spells to bring good fortune. When casting these kinds of spells, you should exercise caution. While there's nothing wrong with casting magic for personal gain, if you do not word your spells and your intent very carefully, you may find you should have been more careful what you wished for. You may wish for a windfall, then find someone passes on and you receive an inheritance. You may wish for a new job, but only receive an interview because their first choice for that job has fallen ill. Make sure your intention is clear, and that the words of your spell cannot be misinterpreted.

Green is the color most commonly associated with luck - it is the color of four-leafed clovers, after all. But gold, with its strong masculine energy and connection to the sun, is often associated with financial prosperity and business success. And orange is connected with confidence, so can be used to work any success spell that calls for increased confidence (such as for a job interview). Basil, as well as being good for protection and in spells of fidelity, is also a useful herb in magical workings to improve your prosperity. Several common spices, including cinnamon, nutmeg, allspice and fennel seeds, also have a strong association with luck and good fortune. As an added bonus, they smell pretty nice - so if you want to carry something around with you to attract luck and wealth, as well as smell fantastic, you could try using these spices. Patchouli is also popularly used in spells for success, but can smell a little less pleasant.

One very popular way of increasing your luck is to carry an acorn, or to place an acorn on your windowsill to bring prosperity to your house. Tonka beans and clover can also be carried, or used in magical workings, to bring success. If you prefer working with crystals, citrine is often used to draw wealth to you, while amber (not technically a crystal) can be used to bring prosperity. Jade has been used for centuries to bring luck and prosperity, and is another good choice (although it can be a little expensive).

A Spell for Growing Wealth

Not a spell to use if you want money fast, but if you are happy for your wealth to increase naturally over time, then this spell is simple yet surprisingly effective.

You will need:

Some coins

A small plant or tree

A trowel

You can either perform this spell outdoors, if you have a garden, or you can used a potted plant. If you are outside, you will be digging a small hole at the base of the plant or tree you have chosen. Oak trees and blackberry bushes are particularly good for this spell. If you are using a potted plant, any indoor plant will do or, for increased effectiveness, try using a basil plant. For the potted plant, you will be digging a small hole at its base (you may be able to dig the hole with your fingers if you don't mind getting dirty).

Dig the hole, then drop one or two coins inside, and say:

As this plant does prosper and flourish

So too my wealth it shall nourish

Precious coins, silver and gold

I give you now to the ground

Return unto me tenfold

My riches abound

Fill the hole in and keep the plant well fed and watered. As the plant grows, you should see your fortunes begin to improve.

A Spell to Attract Money

Another easy way to attract money to you is to make a charm bag. Carry it around with you and you will find that money is drawn to you, and your wealth increases. This spell isn't going to make you a millionaire, but you may find yourself receiving an unexpected windfall.

You will need:

A small green bag (or piece of green fabric)

Clover

Fennel seeds

An acorn

Some money (coins or notes)

Patchouli essential oil

A green ribbon

Holding the coins in your hand, take a moment to imagine money filling your life. Imagine what you would do with a little extra money - perhaps a holiday, or maybe a little house redecoration. Focus on calling money to you as you place each item in the bag. Sprinkle a little patchouli on the outside of the bag and say:

With this charm, I call forth

Riches and wealth, come to me henceforth

Universe, send thy fortune unto me

And it harm none, so mote it be

Seal the bag (either by sewing it shut or tying it with a green ribbon), and carry it with you until money enters your life and the spell is complete.

A Spell to Increase Your Money

If carrying a charm bag around does not appeal to you, you can also try this quick spell to increase your wealth.

You will need:

A green candle

A few dollar bills

Your wallet

Cast this spell during the waxing moon to increase its effectiveness. Light the candle and sit in front of it, holding the money in your hands. Hold the bills out to the flame (but do not set light to them!), and say:

Light of prosperity, shine down on me

I offer up my wealth to thee

Still holding the notes, fold them in half and say:

As I fold these notes, they shall increase

My wealth now shall never cease

Fold the notes in half again, and say:

My fortune doubles with every turn
This prosperity now I shall earn

Fold the notes one more time (this may be difficult), and say:

Universe, take this money I hold
And return it unto me threefold

Take the folded notes and tuck them into your wallet. Over the next few days, you should notice your wealth beginning to increase.

A Spell for Creativity

Want some help creating that best-selling novel? Need a little extra creative boost at work? Know you have a creative masterpiece inside of you but just need some extra inspiration? Try working this spell to free your mind and unleash your inner genius.

You will need:
Carnations
Violets
An orange candle

A heatproof bowl

Some matches or a lighter

Some paper and a pen/pencil

Place the carnations and violets into the bowl. Before lighting the candle, write what you want to achieve on the paper. Do you want to write a novel? Paint a masterpiece? Maybe you'd just like a little extra creativity to help you out at work. Whatever it is, write it down. Once you're ready, place it into the bowl with the flowers. Light the candle. Take a few moments to look into the light and meditate. Look inside yourself to find that little wellspring of creativity, then whisper:

Little fire, little flame

Burning deep inside

Creativity that has no name

Come out now, no need to hide

Taking the candle, carefully light the items in the bowl, one by one. As they begin to burn, speaking louder now, say:

I call to you, inside my heart

Your wisdom unto me impart

Muses of the ancient art

My great masterpiece will now start

You may feel a sudden flash of inspiration. Feel free to write, draw or sketch anything on that piece of paper - you shouldn't waste the inspiration while you still have it. Creativity can be a fickle thing - you may have to repeat this spell again if you feel your inspiration beginning to dry up.

A Spell to Succeed in Exams

This spell doesn't guarantee that you will pass a test - especially if you haven't studied at all - but it can help you to focus, and stop you from making silly little mistakes that might affect your score.

You will need:

An orange candle

The day before your test, take your notes and textbooks into your ritual space. Place these on the ground in front of you, and light the candle. Place your hands upon the notes and close your eyes. Say:

Oh Great Athena, hear my call

Bring unto me the wisdom of the ages

Tomorrow this knowledge I must recall

Help me to remember what is contained within these pages

Now open your eyes, and look at the candle flame.

Mighty Athena, immortal and wise

I beseech of thee, oh powerful one

Keep my mind focused and my eyes on the prize

Let all my hard work not be undone

But bear in mind that Athena probably won't be too keen to help you if you haven't done any work on your own, so make sure you've studied first before you try this!

A Spell for Success in Your Business

If you run your own business, especially if you're just starting out, you may find it difficult to attract customers. This spell can be used to bring customers to you, and is effective whether you are a freelancer working from home, or whether you own your own shop.

You will need:

A citronella candle

A gold candle

A green candle

A business card

If you can't find a citronella candle, you could use one of those mosquito repelling coils, which also contain the essential oil. If you do not have a business card, use something else that can represent your business - if you run a shop, perhaps an item that you sell. If you are a freelance journalist, you could use a pen, for example.

In your place of business, set up the three candles - gold on the left, green to the right, and citronella in the center. Light the gold candle first, and pass the object that represents your business above the flame, saying:

I call now upon the Sun

Mighty God, great fire,

Masculine energy, bless this one

Send my business profits higher

Now light the green candle, and pass your object above the flame. As you do so, say:

Gods of Luck, Gods of Fortune

Let my wealth grow in proportion

Make my business grow

Until the wealth begins to flow

Finally, light the citronella candle, and once more pass your object above the flame. Say:

I call you, those who will make me prosper

Come buy my wares, I have much to offer

Come to me now, I have much to share

My business is open, I do declare

Taking the citronella candle, walk around your place of business (if you work from home, walk around the room where you do most of your work). As you walk, imagine the customers flocking to you, as the scent of the citronella draws them in. Try not to imagine any specific people while you're doing this, just think of a more general customer. You can continue to burn citronella in your place of work if you like - it has a fairly pleasant smell, and will continue to draw customers in even after you've finished casting this spell.

A Spell for a Successful Job Interview

So, you've been invited to a job interview. Feeling nervous? If you're qualified for the job, but afraid that interview nerves might derail your success, you could try casting a little spell to increase your confidence. No spell can guarantee you'll get a job, but if you're feeling just that little bit more self-assured, at least you'll come out of the interview knowing that you gave your best performance, and gave yourself the greatest chance of success.

You will need:

Orange, yellow, and gold string

Before you begin, sit down and meditate. Clear your mind, and visualize a successful interview. How would you act, what would you say? Walk through the whole interview in your mind, and picture yourself calm and confident throughout. Imagine yourself waiting to be called in, but instead of feeling nervous and on edge, you are relaxed and centered. Walk in and shake the interviewer's hand confidently. And when they ask questions, see yourself answering them easily, without becoming flustered. When you have an image of your confident self strongly in your mind, begin to braid the threads. As you braid, say:

I am strong, I am confident

I am smart, I am competent

Let my light shine for all to see

A successful interview I foresee

Continue reciting and braiding the threads until you reach the end, then tie a knot at each end of the braid. Now this thread is charged with the power of your confidence. You can fashion this into a bracelet to wear on your interview day, or simply tuck it into your pocket, but make sure to carry it with you. As you go for your interview, remember that image you had in your mind of a strong, confident you, and you are sure to have a great interview.

A Spell to Find a Job

Searching for a new job, but not having any success? Use this spell to give your job search a little magical boost.

You will need:

Cinnamon

Anise

Allspice

Basil leaves

A copy of your resume

An envelope

Taking the copy of your resume, fold it carefully. As you fold it say:

Success, success, I summon thee

Bring the job that's right for me

A new job is what I need

In my search I must succeed

On this paper I write my skills

Find the job I can fulfill

Slide a few basil leaves into the envelope, and say:

A little luck is what I need

In my search I will succeed

Next, sprinkle the spices into the envelope and say:

I send myself out into the world
And to a job will be referred

Now lick the envelope and seal it shut, saying:

Now to the universe I appeal
And with my essence I seal the deal

Place the envelope somewhere safe until your search is complete and you have a new job. Then you can burn the envelope to end the spell.

A Spell for Success in a New Job

Now that you've found the right job for you, you want to make a good impression. Wait until the new moon, and then cast this simple spell to perform well, impress your new boss, and set yourself up for success in your new job.

You will need:
Allspice
Sage
A bowl of water
Citrine

A white candle

Cast a circle, and arrange your items around the circle as follows: citrine to the North, allspice to the South, sage to the East and the bowl of water to the West. You may want to place the sage and allspice into a bowl to make it easier. Once you have done this, light the white candle. Beginning in the north, take the white candle and allow some of the melting wax to drip onto the citrine. As you do so, say:

Element of Earth, I thank you for my success

I ask you now to bring me prosperity

In my new job, allow me to impress

Let achievement now be a surety

Moving to the east, allow some of the melting wax to drip into the bowl of sage and say:

Element of Air, I thank you for my success

I ask you now, cleanse me of my past mistakes

My new beginnings now to bless

The future I wholeheartedly embrace

Next, move to the south. Let some of the melting wax drip into the bowl of allspice, and say:

Element of Fire, I thank you for my success

I ask you now, give me energy for the future

Bring me the desire, the will to progress

Allow me to reach my potential sooner

Finally, move to the west. As the melting wax drips into the bowl of water, say:

Element of Water, I thank you for my success

I ask you now, wash away that which has passed

My desire for a fresh start to you I now profess

Success and prosperity in my future is forecast

After the spell is finished, you can use the patterns of the wax you've dripped in the water for divination, to see if the new job is right for you, and if you will achieve the success you desire. For now, move back to the center of the circle and say (insert the name of your deities if appropriate):

Goddess, God, I thank you for my success

Allow me to perform to the best of my ability

Give me the chance to impress

Let me demonstrate my capability

In my new job, let me perform well

My success to new heights I shall propel

Now is the time for divination, if you wish to perform it. If not, you can open the circle and go to your new job knowing that you've given your chances of success and prosperity a significant boost.

A Spell to Find Your Dream Job

Perhaps you don't want to find just any old job. Maybe you're looking for your dream job, that one job where you would look forward to going to work every day, where all your skills and talents would be put to good use. This spell is very similar to the one used to find your soulmate - only this time, instead of a person you are trying to find a job that is perfectly matched to you.

You will need:

Some paper, torn into small pieces

A pen or pencil

A windy day

This spell is best cast at the new moon, or you can also cast it at the waxing moon because it is a spell of attraction. Either way, you want to wait for a day with a breeze strong enough to carry your wishes. Take a few moments to think about your perfect job - what would it involve? What would your responsibilities be? Do you know what you'd like your job title to be? What kind of working environment would be ideal?

Write all of these thoughts down on little pieces of paper. Holding them in your hand, stand outside in the wind and say:

Spirits of the air, winged carriers of wishes

I call upon you to see my ambition

Bring me what my soul requires

A job that meets my heart's desires

Work where I can use my expertise

Assignments I complete with ease

Wind, I cast unto you my yearning

In hopes that I will soon be earning

Open your hands and allow the wind to take the pieces of paper from you. Watch as they dance away and know that you are casting your wish out into the universe, and if the time is right, the universe will send you that which you most desire.

A Spell to Bring Happiness

Perhaps the biggest success of all is to be happy in your life. Maybe finding that new job, even if it was your dream job, hasn't quite brought you the happiness you desired. You can also try casting a spell to attract happiness into your life, to make yourself feel a little bit better.

You will need:

Amethyst

Oregano

A bowl

A yellow candle

Light the candle, and place the bowl in front of it. Holding the amethyst in your hands, spend a few moments watching the candle burn and think about what happiness means to you. Remember a time when you felt those positive feelings, when you were the happiest, and charge the crystal with that positive energy. When the amethyst has received as much positive energy as it can hold, place it in the bowl. Taking the oregano, sprinkle it over the amethyst and chant:

Happiness, joy, come to me

Full of laughter I now shall be

Contentment, delight, I summon thee

My happiness now I guarantee

Place the amethyst in a prominent place in your house to bring happiness to your household, or carry it around with you for your own personal happiness. You can also try keeping an oregano plant in your home to attract even more happiness.

Miscellaneous Spells

Because magic can be used for almost any purpose you can imagine, there are many spells that do not fit into the above categories. Here is a small selection of miscellaneous spells - some whimsical, some a little more serious, but they are just as magical as spells cast to bring you job success, or to make your lover faithful. In fact, day to day these spells may be a little more practical - finding a new job is (hopefully) something you won't have to do very often, but running late for work may well be a daily occurrence.

Because these spells are for everyday use, they are designed to be quick and easy, and as such require very few ingredients. If you're casting a spell to find where you've parked your car, you don't want to have to go to the local shop to buy some herbs first. You just want to cast your spell, find your car, and then move on.

A Spell to Find Lost Items

Everyone loses things from time to time, but when you've been searching for a while and been having no luck, or if you need to find your item in a hurry, try using this quick little spell.

You will need:

Your willpower

Take a moment to think about the item you are missing. Imagine what it looks like, and keep that image strongly in your mind as you say:

Spirits of nature, elemental power

For many hours I have looked, my home I have scoured

I ask for your help, bring my (item) back to me

As I will, so mote it be

You will be surprised at how well this spell works. The next place you look, you will find the item that you seek.

A Spell to Find Where You Parked Your Car

After a long day at work, you've come back to the parking lot only to find that your mind has gone totally blank - you have no idea where you've parked your car. Before you start walking up and down rows in a desperate hunt, try casting this little spell to point you in the right direction.

You will need:

Your willpower

Your car keys

Hold your car keys out and allow them to dangle, like you would if you were using a pendulum. Visualize your car, and allowing the keys to hang freely, say:

North, South, East, West

Show me now the way that's best

My car's location is unclear

Is it far or is it near?

Earth, Fire, Water, Air

Take me now over there

The keys should now indicate to you in which direction you should walk. If they don't, maybe you're on the wrong floor of the parking garage. Move to another floor and try again.

A Spell to Calm Your Anger

It's very easy to let the little things wind you up. Sometimes it helps to take a step back and to take a few deep breaths, but if you find you're still struggling to let go of your anger, try using this spell.

You will need:

A smooth rock

Running water (such as a river)

Holding the rock in your hands, take a few moments to feel your anger. Let it fill you, then feel the cool smoothness of the rock in your hands and imagine your anger transferring to the rock. Imagine that the rock is as full of anger as you once were. Now place the rock into the river. As the water runs over it, imagine the water is taking that anger away, washing it downstream. Feel the cooling power of the water on your own anger, and as it begins to dissipate you should say:

Cool water, running river

I feel your heart, steady and calm

I feel you sooth me like a balm

Take my anger, let me see clearer

Remove this poison from my heart

Your tranquility unto me impart

If you like, you can meditate for a while - watching running water has a wonderfully calming effect. When you feel more relaxed, go back to your everyday life but hold the river's tranquility inside your heart, and feel it continuing to work to cool your anger.

A Spell for When You're at a Crossroads in Life

Sometimes in life, you find yourself with an important, potentially life-changing decision to make. Maybe you've been offered your dream job, but to take it would mean moving away from your friends and family and starting a new life for yourself. Perhaps you're wondering if you should stay in a career you find unfulfilling, or take a chance and make the jump to a new career. Or perhaps you have a good job, and a potential career, but you're considering taking a year out to go traveling. Decisions are difficult, but major decisions like these can take a lot of thought, and unsurprisingly many people seek guidance when they are faced with such a tough choice.

Now, more than ever, is the time to seek advice from the deities, to let the universe point you in the right direction. Of course, it's still your own choice - you can add the advice you receive from this spell to your list of pros and cons when it comes to making your decision. But it still doesn't hurt to ask for a little bit of guidance. This spell calls upon Hecate, who guards all crossroads (both physical and metaphorical), but you can also feel free to pray to your own patron deities for a little extra advice.

You will need:

A black candle

A piece of paper and pen/pencil

This spell is best performed at the dark of the moon, and at night time. On the piece of paper write the choice you are facing. You don't need to write too much detail - just something like "Should I take this new job I have been offered, or should I stay in my old job?" Once you have done that, light the candle, and say:

Hecate, Mother Goddess, Crone

My path into the future is unknown

For such a decision is too big to make alone

I have found a crossroads in my way

I must make a decision without delay

For your help, Hecate, I humbly pray

The way forward is out of sight

Should I turn left, or turn to the right?

Hecate I ask for your help in this plight

Now burn the piece of paper in the candle flame. When you wake up in the morning, the way forward will be clear to you. You may have a dream showing you the choice you should make, or you may simply wake up knowing with an unshakeable certainty what you need to do next.

A Spell to Fix Something That's Broken

Now, this isn't a spell to use if you've thrown a ball through your kitchen window. But if your TV isn't working properly and you don't know why, try this little spell to see if you can fix it.

You will need:

A piece of string

Standing in front of the thing that is broken, hold the string firmly in both hands, concentrate, and say:

Gremlins, glitches, I cast you out

You're unwelcome here, have no doubt

In this string I bind these troubles

The lifespan of my (item) doubles

Tie a firm knot in the piece of string. If the item is still not working, try casting the spell again, and tying another knot in the string. If it still doesn't work, then it might be time to call the repairman.

If your car won't start, you can try a similar spell. Holding the piece of string in your hands, focus your mind and say:

I am late, no time to wait

This car must start, so I may depart

Tie a firm knot in the piece of string, and your car should start. If it doesn't, try again. If it still doesn't work, it might be time to take your car to the garage.

A Spell for When You're Running Late

You've slept through the alarm again, rushing out the door without even time for a cup of coffee, and now it seems like you're hitting every red light between here and the office! What are you going to do? You might think there's not much beyond crossing your fingers, cursing at the lights, and vowing never to oversleep again, but while you're waiting, why not try casting a little spell and see if you can make those lights turn to green.

You will need:

Your willpower

As you are sitting in traffic, focus on the red light ahead of you and say:

Oh light that impedes my journey

Change to green so I may be early

Let nothing more stand in my way

Bring me to the office without delay!

Focus on releasing the energy, and imagine every light ahead of you changing to green. This may work, this may not - after all, there may be another Wiccan driving the other way casting the same spell! - but it's always worth a try. And it gives you something to keep your mind occupied while you wait.

A Spell for Dream Divination

If you've tried the crossroads decision-making spell, you've already practiced a form of dream divination. But divination doesn't have to only be used for life-altering decisions; it can be used any time you have a question, or would like a little bit of advice.

You will need:

A blue bag (or piece of fabric)

Bay leaf

Cinnamon

Star anise

Orange peel

Caraway seeds

A silver ribbon

Before you place the herbs and spices into the bag, you should think about the question you want answered. Or maybe you would just like some general advice on a particular area in your life. Whatever it is, make sure that the question is clear in your mind. Remember, intention and focus is everything when it comes to spellcasting, and even more so when you are performing divination. When you're sure you know what you want to ask, place the items one by one into the bag and say:

Morpheus, keeper of dreams

Grant to me clear sight

In my dreams now send a sign

Hermes, messenger of the divine

Show me the truth this night

Tell me what the answer means

Tie the bag shut and place it underneath your pillow. When you awaken, write down your dreams in your Book of Shadows. The answer to your question will be in the dream, and you just have to interpret and understand what is being said.

How to Become a Successful Spellcaster

If you want to become a more proficient spellcaster, the most important thing is to have belief in yourself and in your abilities. Magic thrives on belief. If you don't believe that the spell you are casting is going to work, then the energy you are directing toward your goal is naturally a bit weaker - and sometimes it's that little bit that makes all the difference. When you first start practicing magic, it may seem hard to believe that sprinkling some herbs and saying a few words can bring to you what you desire. But trust in the universe. If your aim is clear, and your intention is pure, then that spell will work. It may not work in the way you expect - the universe has a way of bringing us what we need most, not just what we want - but it will work.

But try to give the universe a little helping hand. Don't cast a spell to find romance and then sit at home watching TV. How are you going to meet anyone if you don't get out there and try? Magic can give you a little extra boost, but you've got to be moving in the right direction to start with. Don't cast a job spell then sit there twiddling your thumbs and waiting for something to happen. Keep networking, keep sending your CVs out, keep your eyes open for that perfect job that the universe will send your way.

You should also practice reading spells fluidly. Words have power, and if your recitation isn't clear, and you're stumbling over words, the spell may be less powerful. Practice reading the spell until you have it clear in your mind, before you actually cast it. The spells should roll off your tongue without hesitation. All spells have a natural rhythm - find it, and you will be a proficient spellcaster in no time.

You also need to learn how to clear your mind. For most people, their minds are crowded with thoughts, and it can be difficult to concentrate on just one thing. But magic requires a huge amount of focus, and you need to be able to concentrate while casting a spells, without your mind wandering off to what you're going to cook for dinner. For many people, meditating provides an efficient way to learn this focus. You might be thinking "Meditation isn't for me. I can't just sit there and think of nothing!" But just try it. Spend a few minutes sitting and focusing on your breathing - in and out, in and out. Thoughts will pop into your mind, but don't dwell on them. Just let them pass through your mind as you continue to focus on your breathing. Just like magic, with practice meditation becomes easier and easier, and before too long you will find it easier to focus your mind on your breathing, and not allow your thoughts to distract you. You can then apply that same focus to your spellcasting, clearing your mind and focusing on your intentions before beginning to cast any spell.

As you continue to practice, you may feel that you want to try writing your own spells. The more you practice magic, the easier this becomes - you will get a feel for what herbs work for which kinds of magic and for how you should arrange your crystals. The hardest part of any spell comes in writing the words. Spells don't have to rhyme, but rhyming can help give them that natural rhythm that makes them easier to cast. Spells should also be worded carefully - remember, words have power, and using the wrong words can have consequences. When you are writing a spell, take your time. Don't rush, and you will find that the right words come to you naturally. If you cast your spell, and it doesn't work, don't fret - look at it again, tweak the words a little, maybe add a few extra ingredients. And then try again. It takes practice to become a proficient spellcaster, and even the best spellcasters have trouble writing spells sometimes. But don't give up - eventually you will write a spell that just clicks, and you'll feel the boost in power and confidence that comes with knowing that you have created your own magic.

The energy of the universe is powerful - learn how to control and direct that energy, to meet your goals and achieve your desires. Just always remember to harm none, to have faith, and to concentrate, and you are well on your way to being a successful spellcaster.

Blessed be!

Finally, if you enjoyed this book, then I'd like to ask you for a favor, would you be kind enough to leave a review for this book on Amazon?

It'd be greatly appreciated!

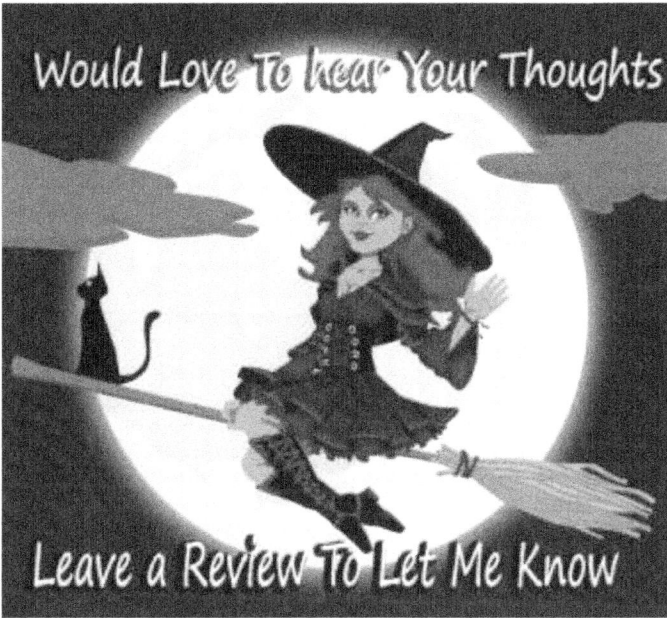

Would Love To hear Your Thoughts

Leave a Review To Let Me Know

Thank you and good luck!

Free Essential Magick Book

Wicca Magick can be a difficult subject to grasp, luckily I have give you many books to get your head around it.

Gain more knowledge! Grab your FREE copy of The Essential Magick Book to help you understand what you need to be a better practitioner

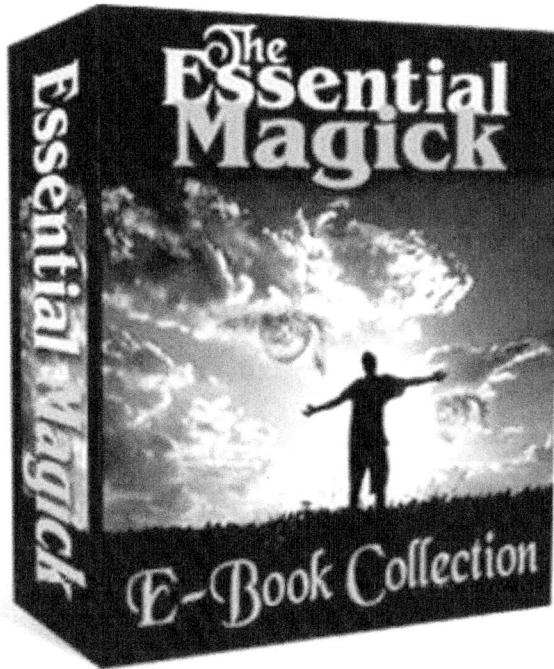

To grab your copy of The Marketing Blue Print visit

http://www.scarlettwrightbooks.com/wiccamagick

Printed in Great Britain
by Amazon